100
PLAYS
FOR THE FIRST
HUNDRED DAYS

Books by Suzan-Lori Parks
Available from TCG

The America Play and Other Works

Also Includes:

Betting on the Dust Commander
The Death of the Last Black Man in the Whole Entire World
Devotees in the Garden of Love
Imperceptible Mutabilities in the Third Kingdom
Pickling
Essays

The Book of Grace

Father Comes Home from the Wars (Parts 1, 2 & 3)

100 Plays for the First Hundred Days

The Red Letter Plays

Includes:

Fucking A
In the Blood

365 Days/365 Plays

Topdog/Underdog

Venus

100 PLAYS FOR THE FIRST HUNDRED DAYS

Suzan-Lori Parks

Theatre Communications Group
New York
2018

100 Plays for the First Hundred Days is published by
Theatre Communications Group, Inc., 520 Eighth Avenue,
24th Floor, New York, NY 10018-4156

The publication of *100 Plays for the First Hundred Days* by Suzan-Lori Parks, through TCG's Book Program, is made possible in part by the New York State Council on the Arts with the support of Governor Andrew Cuomo and the New York State Legislature.

TCG books are exclusively distributed to the book trade by Consortium Book Sales and Distribution.

ISBN 978-1-55936-584-0 (paperback)
ISBN 978-1-55936-899-5 (ebook)

A catalog record for this book is available from the Library of Congress.

Book design and composition by Lisa Govan
Cover design by Rodrigo Corral and Sungpyo Hong
Cover photo by Alexis Capitini

First Edition, May 2018

For Durham and Christian and Stephanie and Mom
and also, for all of us.

Contents

Preface

I wrote this for all of us. No matter who you voted for. If you voted for her or him. If you didn't vote. For whatever your reason. Maybe you weren't yet old enough. Maybe you had better things to do. Maybe you don't even live in this country. Maybe you don't even care. Still, I wrote this for all of us. I woke up every day and I read the news and I wrote a play. It sounds easy. Trust me, it was hard. For those of you who aren't familiar with my work, a-play-a-day-writing as a way to meditate, as a way to pray, is a thing I've done before. These plays are a reach across the aisle. A dive into the mosh pit. They're a way to hold a mirror up to nature, like Hamlet suggested. They're full of hope and rage and humor and despair and joy and astonishment and pride and disbelief and they were the best way, during those first 100 days of our new era, as our new president was elected on the promise that he will make us all great again, well, bearing witness and writing these plays was the best way I knew how to stay woke.

Xoxox, SLP

New York City
March 2018

From the Author's Elements of Style

I'm continuing the use of my slightly unconventional theatrical elements. Here's a road map.

- *(Rest)*
  Take a little time, a pause, a breather; make a transition.

- A Spell
  An elongated and heightened *(Rest)*. Denoted by repetition of figures' names with no dialogue. Has sort of an architectural look:

  Someone
  Someone Else
  Someone
  Someone Else

This is a place where the figures experience their pure true simple state. While no action or stage business is necessary, directors should fill this moment as they best see fit.

- "/" indicates overlapping dialogue.

100 PLAYS FOR THE FIRST HUNDRED DAYS

Day 1: January 20

IS IT OVER YET?

A very bright room. Someone sits, eyes closed tightly.
Perhaps fingers in their ears too.
Someone Else joins them.

Someone Else
It's Inauguration Day.

Someone
I know that.

Someone Else
I voted for Her.

Someone
Me too.

Someone Else
She didn't win.

Someone
Are you rubbing it in?

Someone Else
Nope. Just. Stating a fact.

Someone
That's refreshing these days. A fact. A fact that's true.

Someone Else
We totally blew it. Giving new meaning to "it's my party and I'll cry if I want to."

Someone
That's funny.

Someone Else
You can totally hear me.

Someone
Yep.

Someone Else
Then why are you plugging your ears?

Someone
I'll unplug them.

Someone Else
And open your eyes.

Someone
Nope. Can't bear to look. Can't bear to watch.

Someone Else
Ok.

Someone
Is it over yet?

Someone Else
Nope.

Someone
Are we "great again" yet?

Someone Else
Nope.

Someone
I want to cry.

Someone Else
Let's cry together.

They cry together. Ugly tears.

Someone Else
Better? Even a little?

Someone
Nope. I'm angry. Very.

Someone Else
Me too.

They yell and scream and gnash their teeth.
Very real.

Someone Else
Better?

Someone
Not really.

(Rest)

Someone
Is it over yet?

Someone Else
It's Inauguration Day. 5 A.M. They're—they're just getting started.

Someone
Someone Else

Someone Else
Just a question: Are you gonna keep your eyes shut for the next 4 years?

Someone
I'm planning on it.

Day 2: January 21

MARCHING

Someone is marching in place.
Someone Else is holding a large stack of posterboard.

Someone Else
What are you doing?

Someone
I'm marching.

Someone Else
Marching in protest?

Someone
That's right.

Someone Else
Right on. What's the message?

Someone
Presence is the protest. My body will be among the ones counted.

Someone Else
You're marching with your eyes closed.

Someone
I'm showing up.

Someone Else
Right on.

Someone Else holds up a sign. It can read anything appropriate:
Not My President.
Love Trumps Hate.
Radical Inclusion.

Someone
What are you doing?

Someone Else
Holding up signs.

Someone
What do they say?

Someone Else
Someone Else

At last Someone opens their eyes.
Looks. Keeps their eyes open.
And Someone Else marches with them.

Day 3: January 22

ALT FACTS

Someone still marching. Someone Else still showing signs.
Or maybe at this point Someone Else is just shouting slogans.
Free-form in the vein of whatever is appropriate.
Then Spokesperson enters.

Spokesperson
The world is flat.

Someone
Lies!

Spokesperson
The sun revolves around the earth.

Someone Else
Lies, yo!

Spokesperson
There were more people at Friday's inauguration than at the 2 inaugurations previous. Combined.

Someone and Someone Else
Lies!

Spokesperson
And you know what's really great? There were more folks at the 45th's inauguration than at that "Women's March" yesterday.

Someone and Someone Else
LIES!

Spokesperson
"Alternative Facts." We don't call them "lies." We don't call them "falsehoods." We call them "Alternative Facts." So there.

Someone
Someone Else
Spokesperson
Someone Else
Someone

(Rest)

The Spokesperson exits. Perhaps pursued by a bear. Like in that Shakespeare play. Or maybe the Spokesperson just exits. Someone and Someone Else are filled with rage. Imagine the rage of the popular vote in the shadow of the electoral college. It's slasher. It's epic. It's—over. Someone and Someone Else are covered with blood.

Someone
So there.

Someone Else
Yup.

Someone
Someone Else

Someone Else
Wake up!

Someone and Someone Else freeze.
The real Someone Else and Someone come onstage.

Someone Else
Wake up!

Someone
Right. We were just having /

Someone Else
/ A joint dream /

Someone
It happens?

Someone Else
Yep. We were asleep. We had a dream. You woke?

Someone
I'm woke. Now what?

Day 4: January 23

HONERED TO SERVE

The 45th
"I am honered to serve you, the great American people, as your 45th President of the United States."

Someone
You spelled "honored" wrong, Mr. President. In your tweet. You misspelled it, then you deleted it, and it appeared later spelled correctly. I'm just saying.

2 Goons rush in and remove Someone.

Day 5: January 24

WATCHING TV

The 45th watching TV. A lot of it.
News shows and talk shows.
The Spokesperson is standing by.

Various News Sources
The inauguration crowds were smaller than those of the 44th President.

The 45th
Go tell them my crowds were big.

Spokesperson
(Yelling) His crowds were big.

The 45th
Go tell them. Tell them that they were bigger than the 44th's and bigger than anyone else's ever.

Spokesperson
(Yelling) They were the biggest. Ever.

The 45th
Shout it from the highest mountain or something.

Spokesperson
You got it.

The 45th
"When I gave my speech, I looked out . . . and saw like a million people."*

Spokesperson
You said that when you spoke with the CIA.

The 45th
Do you think they bought it?

Spokesperson
They're the CIA.

The 45th
I don't care if they don't believe me. The people believe me. What are you standing there for? Go tell them.

Spokesperson goes.

Someone Else
What's he doing?

Another One
Watching TV. Like. A lot of it.**

The 45th
"Because I'm like a smart guy."*

* Actual 45th President's words.
** Actual 45th President's activities.

Day 6: January 25

THE SIGNAGE

Oval Office. The 45th sits at his desk surrounded by white men in suits, or actors holding signs reading "I'm Playing the Part of a White Man" in front of their faces. The 45th signs something then hands it to the Vice President.

The 45th
I've just given the pipelines a green light again. They'll ruin the environment and disrupt so-called "native" lands but they'll put money in the pockets of people who already have a lot of money.

He signs something else.

The 45th
I've just re-imposed the gag order on women's reproductive rights and health care. The only thing we want to do is dump our sperm into women. After that—really, we don't care. No health care, no child support, no funding for schools, but if they don't want the child, they gotta have the child 'cause the child is a creation of God, and, you get the gist, give me something else to sign.

He signs something else.

The 45th
I'm signing other things. Horrible things. Believe it.

Someone Else watches with Another.
They're watching it all on TV.

Another
I hear he's addicted to television.

Someone Else
Yep.

Another
What happened to your friend?

Someone Else
They got taken away.

Another
I admire the use of the "they" and "them" when referring to them—'cause they could be cast as any gender and—

Someone Else
Yeah. They could be dead. But, yeah.

Another
No word?

Someone
Nope.

Another
The Fall of America.

Someone
Huh?

Another
That's what this show is called. It's the reality show of the century.

Someone
You think he watches it?

Another
You betcha.

They keep watching.
The 45th keeps signing things.
It's grim.

Day 7: January 26

THE DIVIDING LINE

The 45th
I'm signing a bill to ban Muslims from entering our beautiful and important country.

Someone enters. Haggard but still alive.

The 45th
I'm signing a bill to get that wall built between us and Mexico. 'Cause, what's a country without a border?

Someone
"Good fences make good neighbors."

Someone Else
Did August Wilson say that?

Someone
Robert Frost. Ironically. Is he for real?

Someone Else
Is that a trick question? Welcome back. You ok?

Someone
I'm here.

Someone Else
Where did they take you when they took you away?

Someone
They took me into the future.

Someone Else
They can do that?

Someone
They're Feds.

Someone Else
Right. How'd it look?

Someone
Good.

Someone Else
Really?

Someone
Yep. Believe it.

Someone gets up.

Someone Else
Where are you going?

Someone
There's a love rally in Washington Square Park.

Someone Else
Let's go.

Day 8: January 27

DOING THE MATH

Y
We're one week in. Day 8.

X
Yep.

Y
What are you doing?

X
I'm doing the Math.

Y
The what?

X
The Math: Am I or am I not one of the people who is or who will eventually be, at some point in the near future, targeted by him and his people? And if I am or will be, then how many people or types of people will be targeted before me/my type? How long do I have to get packed? What, if any, countries/cities/towns will welcome me/my type? Will my movement alert them or others? Basically, do I have a chance in hell?

Y
There were some people in the coffee shop just now talking about almost the same thing. Telling each other why they'd be "ok" or why they wouldn't.

X
It's come to this so quickly. Will we be, in the not so distant future, one of those historical episodes. Like when you see photographs from, say, someplace in the '70s or—you know what I mean. There are places that are totally bombed-out now and you see a photo of that place, taken not too long ago, back when in that place life was good. Back when people who lived there lived in a center of world culture and then, well, things changed.

Y
There's always Mars. We could go there.

X
Or we could stay here and just drink and fuck and get high and say fuck it.

Y
That is always an option.

Day 9: January 28

IS SHE JEWISH? / ARE THEY MUSLIM?

X
Is she Jewish?

Y
We used to play that game. To feel solidarity with movie stars we would watch TV and ask each other: "Who's the Jew?"

X
Ivanka? Jewish?

Y
Good question.

X
There's a group of rabbis. They're having a meeting. They want to make an exception. To curry favor with her dad.

Y
Jeez.

X
Meanwhile. Refugees and nice folks from Iraq are being detained at JFK Airport.

Y
Are they Muslim?

X
Good question. Maybe.

Y
Jeez.

Day 10: January 29

SMALL HANDS

Ben
Look at all those Executive Orders he's signing.

Franklin
Yeah.

Tom
He has such small hands.

Jefferson
Yeah.

Day 11: January 30

2 BROTHERS*

Brother 1
“It’s just been one week. We need to give him a chance.”

Brother 2
“If a Muslim woman wants to move here. Fine. But she should leave her towel at home.”

Brother 1
“’Cause this is a Christian country.”

Brother 2
“That’s why it’s a great country.”

Brother 1
“I wanted Hillary in the worst way. But I didn’t vote. I had a chance to have a say and I didn’t say. So now I don’t have a chance to say.”

Someone
“Say what?”

* Overheard conversation.

Day 12: January 31

SLIM PICKINGS

Someone
He’s picking his Supreme Court nominee tonight. Announcing it on TV. Prime-time live. Hoping he gets a ratings surge. What are you doing?

Y
I’m picking my nose.

Day 13: February 1

HAPPY BLACK HISTORY MONTH

The 45th
Happy Black History Month. I've scheduled a whole month of events starting with a Listening Breakfast where I'm surrounded by my Negroes and they smile at me while I say things like: "Frederick Douglass is a great guy. He says and does great things."*

Y
He's using the present tense to talk about Frederick Douglass.

X
Are we still having Black History Month?

Y
Not for long. Enjoy it while we can.

House Negro
Mr. 45th, gang leaders in Chicago want to sit down with you 'cause they know you're for real, not like the last president.

X
Some black folks will only say what white folks want them to say. Post-Traumatic Slave Disorder.

Y
I wanna cry me a river.

X
I wanna slap me somebody.

* Not an actual quote but close.

Day 14: February 2

EERIE 'CAUSE I WANNA

X
Now I'm worried.

Y
Because he's threatening to send troops to Mexico to help them deal with their "bad hombres"?

X
No.

Y
Because he's alienating Japan, Germany and Australia?

X
No. How do you alienate Australia?

Y
What's got you worried?

X
I'm realizing that I have a gap in my armor. I'm recognizing my own Achilles' heel. He had that Listening Breakfast meeting with those black folks.

Y
They're Uncle Toms every single one of them, and they're assholes.

X
Still they're black.

Y
Your point?

X
I felt glad. I felt, well, at least he's meeting with them. At least he's talking with us.

Y
Woah—

X
That's why I'm worried. 'Cause I don't like him. I don't respect him. I feel he is a great shame and a disservice but—I *want* to like him. That's what I feel. My shortcoming. My Achilles' heel. I *want* to like our president. And I'm scared because I'm weak like that.

Y
Hold me.

They hug.

Day 15: February 3

CRAY-CRAY

Another
I just heard that the 45th lifted the ban on the mentally insane being able to purchase firearms.

Someone
So *crazy* people can now buy guns no problem.

Another
Yep.

Someone
I wonder how that's gonna go?

On the sidewalk a Woman with a leashless Pug dog passes by a Man Wearing Earphones.

Man Wearing Earphones
PUT YOUR DOG ON A LEASH!!

Woman with Pug
HE DOESN'T NEED ONE!!

Another
Cray-cray.

Someone
Yep.

Day 16: February 4

SAMO

Y
Homeland Security refuses to enforce the ban.

X
And a judge blocked it.

The 45th
I'm tweeting "Make America Great Again."

Z
Ain't he got nothing else?

Day 17: February 5

NOT YET BROKE

X
We're 2 weeks in.

Y
I'm taking a break from it.

X
Bill O'Reilly says Putin's a killer and the 45th is like:
"What, you think our country's so innocent?"

Y
I'm going on vacation.

X
An appeals court rejected the request to reinstate the Muslim ban.

Y
I wanna go to a sunny beach and put my head in the sand.

X
Melissa McCarthy played Sean Spicer on *SNL*.

Y
Yes.

Day 18: February 6

VENUS AND SERENA

The Writer writes.

The Writer
Dear Mr. Baldwin:
Here again at Watch Me Work. With this beautiful group of lovely writers and artists. And I wanna write the play of the day but I don't got a clue, have not had time to listen to the news. The first 2 weeks:
Day 1: Inauguration.
Day 2: He goes to the CIA and talks about how his crowd size was just as big or bigger than Obama's—even though all sources say that the 45th's crowds were teeny. He's lying out his ass to the fucking CIA.
Day 3: That was the day when Kellyanne called lies "alternative facts."
Day 4: Was the day that he said he was gonna investigate the voter fraud.

(Although nobody 'cept him thinks there was any. And several of his key people are registered to vote in more than one state.)
Day 5: He gave the Dakota Pipeline the thumbs-up so that's happening again. Jeez.
Day 6: He promised to repeal Obamacare and said some shit about Mexico, and so the President of Mexico canceled his visit here. And he also gave a thumbs-up to waterboarding.
Day 7: He signs the anti-Muslim ban.
Day 8: Angry crowds in the street protest the anti-Muslim ban. He calls several foreign leaders, insulting folks in Australia.
Day 9: A U.S. Navy Seal is killed during a raid in Yemen, several civilians killed as well. Protests continue at airports over the Muslim ban.
Day 10: He fires Sally Yates, an Acting Attorney General, 'cause she speaks out against the ban.
Day 11: He nominates Gorsuch to fill the SCOTUS seat.
Day 12: He says he will send troops to Mexico to stop the "bad hombres" down there.
Day 13: During the remarks at the National Prayer Breakfast, he bad-mouths Arnold Schwarzenegger for his low ratings on the TV show *Celebrity Apprentice*.
Day 14: A federal judge bans his Muslim ban. The judge's ban is effective nationwide. Yay.
Day 15: Trump tweets that a lot of bad folks will be coming into the country because of the ban being rescinded.

X
That's the first 2 weeks.

Y
But it's not a play.

X
Why not?

Y
Because it doesn't have a beginning middle and end.

X
So what?

Y
It doesn't have an arc of development.

X
So what?

Y
The characters, if any, don't change. There aren't any beats, it's just a writer copying the news, just regurgitating the vomit.

X
I know what would make it a play.

Y
What?

X
Venus and Serena.

Y
?

X slaps Y. First forehand then backhand.

Y
That hurt. A lot.

X
These are desperate times. Sorry.

Day 19: February 7

DOWNHILL

M

Betsy DeVos got confirmed for Education Secretary. Pence cast the tiebreaking vote.

N

I'm sending love to all the folks who stood up against her.

O

Here's a list of the ones who voted for her and you can see how her family sent each of them a substantial financial contribution.

M

Army Corps of Engineers is going ahead with the Dakota Pipeline.

N

I'm sending love to the folks who stood up against it.

O

Here's a list of the recent oil spills and environmental disasters. Including the one in the Midwest that is not being reported on.

M

Elizabeth Warren, speaking against Jeff Sessions, read a letter from Coretta Scott King in which Mrs. King spoke about how Jeff Sessions intimidated black and poor voters. And, while speaking against Sessions, Ms. Warren was told by Mitch McConnell to sit down and stop speaking.

O

Nevertheless she persisted.

B

These plays—these plays are really going downhill.

X
As a representative of the playwright I'm telling you—

B
What?

X holds his head in his hands. No words.

Day 20: February 8

SHUT UP

Elizabeth Warren
I'm Elizabeth Warren and, as part of the confirmation hearing of Jeff Sessions for Attorney General, I'm reading a letter from the widow of Dr. Martin Luther King, Jr., Coretta Scott King.

Mitch McConnell
Shut up.

Elizabeth Warren
What?

Mitch McConnell
Shut up. Everybody who wants her to shut up say shut up.

GOP
Shut up.

X
They confirmed Jeff Sessions as Attorney General.

Y
And a black senator from somewhere, my mind is going blank perhaps as a protective measure, some black senator, wrote letters in Sessions' defense.

X
Shut up. Just. Shut up.

Day 21: February 9

BUY HER STUFF

Spokesperson
Buy Ivanka's stuff! Yeah, I'm working for the White House, but I'm giving a free commercial. Buy her stuff, folks! I don't care if you don't have a job. Or can't afford it. That's what credit cards are for. Buy Ivanka's stuff.*

A
This isn't a play yet.

B
As if that matters.

A
You need to rewrite it. Where are you going?

B
I'm going shopping. Of course.

* These words are an approximation.

Day 22: February 10

EVERYBODY IS FULL OF SHIT, SOME PEOPLE ARE ASSHOLES

May
Kanye was a big supporter of the 45th.

June
Was?

May
Yeah, when 45th didn't invite Kanye to perform at his inauguration, Kanye took down all those positive tweets he wrote. This proves that Mr. West is full of shit.

June
Everybody is full of shit. Some people are assholes. Shit passes but the only thing an asshole will pass is gas.

Day 23: February 11

GOLDEN SHOWERS

July
Did you hear the news? President 45th likes golden showers?

May
That is so not true!

August
What's a golden shower?

July
It's when someone pees on him. He likes Russian hookers to pee on him.

August
The 45th President likes Russian hookers to pee on him?

May
That is like so not true! Right?

July
That's the news.*

August
Guess the 45th is into *world pees* after all. Get it: *world pees—world pees*—World Peace.

They double high-5.

* Could be alt facts.

Day 24: February 12

HOW MANY MORE DAYS OF THIS?

Joker
Happy Lincoln's Birthday!

Penguin
45th is hosting Abe at Mar-a-Lago.

Joker
"Ah-bey"—the Japanese Prime Minister. That's how you pronounce his name.

Penguin
Oh my bad.

Joker
How many more days of this?

Penguin
Don't ask, man.

Day 25: February 13

TOP SECRET

Joe
How do you like this place?

Janet
It's super fancy.

Joe
Happy almost Valentine's Day.

Janet
Can we afford this? The entrées are so pricey.

Joe
I won dinner for two, as in you and me, at the raffle in the office—the holiday party. Surprise.

Janet
You're the best.

Joe
It's a little weird now 'cause—

Janet
'Cause the 45th owns it—

Joe
Mar-a-Lago.

Janet
We are going to enjoy ourselves.

Joe
Regardless.

Janet
Hon, isn't that him? The 45th?

Joe
Where?

Janet
Right there, like at that center table next to that Japanese guy?

Joe
What are they doing eating here?

Janet
Well, I guess he can eat anywhere.

Waiter
He's having a top secret meeting with the Japanese Prime Minister.

Joe
Out in the open? A top secret meeting out in the open?

Waiter
The 45th promised to shake things up.

Janet
On my phone. CNN. Says Korea just test-fired some missiles or something.

Joe
And look—the 45th's phone is ringing and everybody around him is scrambling.

Janet
I'm going to take his picture.

She does.

Joe
I recorded the substance of their meeting. I recorded their voices.

Janet
Because you're a spy.

Joe
Exactly.

Janet
For North Korea?

Joe
Exactly.

Janet
Shit, Joe.

Joe
Exactly.

Day 26: February 14

IN LIKE FLYNN

Speed
In like Flynn.

Top
Flynn got fired.

Speed
Word?

Top
National Security Adviser Flynn got fired 'cause he talked to the Russians and then he lied about it, forgetting that all those conversations are like recorded.

Speed
A bright light for Valentine's Day. I hope.

Day 27: February 15

RICK CARRIES THE FOOTBALL

Mar-a-Lago Guest
Here's Rick. There's the football. The nuclear football. Say hello, Rick.

Rick
Man, you can't tell them that.

Mar-a-Lago Guest
I'm telling the world, Rick. You're a black guy and you are carrying the briefcase that contains the nuclear codes.

Rick
Sir please—

Mar-a-Lago Guest
And I am telling the world! Because, I mean, this is fun right?

Rick
Shit. Shit. Shit.

Smith
This really happened. Now we all know who is carrying the nuclear codes.

Jones
Shit.

Day 28: February 16

RED STATE, BLUE STATE, DEEP STATE

Redneck
A redneck is often from a red state and we're like conservatives.

Blueneck
Or racists.

Redneck
Not always but sometimes. Yep.

Blueneck
A blueneck is from a blue state. And we are progressives.

Redneck
Or liberal losers?

Blueneck
Not always but sometimes. Yep.

Redneck
I'm packing. A gun.

Blueneck
Thank you for the information.

Deepneck
A deepneck is from a deep state.

Rednecks and Bluenecks
Huh?

Deepneck
Deep states are those of us who are enmeshed deep in the government, regardless of who is elected. We're the CIA, FBI, NSI, the Spooks, the Spies. We run the shit. And make no mistake. We are in control.

Redneck
I'm packing. A gun.

Deepneck snaps his fingers and two hooded folks come in and escort Redneck away.

Blueneck
So, you're on my side?

Deepneck
Not exactly.

Day 29: February 17

NATIONAL GUARD

AP News
The National Guard will be used to round up people who are undocumented residents.

The 45th
That's 100% false. The media is out to get me. The media is the *enemy of the people*. I'm holding like a 77-minute solo

press conference to rant about how I got more votes than any president ever, how I'm going back on the campaign trail 'cause, well it's easier than the job I've campaigned for and how the media is full of lies.

AP News and Many Other Sources
The current administration *did* suggest that the National Guard be deployed as an illegal immigrant roundup force.

The 45th
Ok, so it was a bad idea.

Doc
Why didn't he just say so? That it was a bad idea?

Spock
Dunno, man.

Doc
Doctors are suggesting he get a mental-health check.

Doc holds his breath.

Spock
Don't hold your breath, man.

The 45th continues.

Day 30: February 18

ENEMY OF THE PEOPLE

Stalin
The press is the Enemy of the People!

Mao
The press is the Enemy of the People!

The 45th
The press is the Enemy of the People!

Joe
See any correlation?

Moe
Yeah, the press spews lies, man.

Joe
Oh, man.

Day 31: February 19

SWEDISH MEATBALLS

The 45th
And all the terrorist attacks going on in Sweden—

Swedish People
WTF? Lies lies lies!

Day 32: February 20

PRE-SNOT

A
Pre-snot! Pre-snot! Pre-snot!

B
You mean Pres-not, as in "Happy Not My Presidents' Day."

A
Thanks, man! Pres-not! Pres-not! Pres-not!

Day 33: February 21

DON KING AND DON TRUMP

Several years ago when they were pals and they had almost the same name and both had remarkable hair.

Don King
Hi, I'm Don King. And I love me some Don Trump. You can love Trump and you're still a nigger. Woops.

Don Trump
The crowd watching me watching you is smiling.

Don King
Ok by you?

Don Trump
Ok by me.

Joe
Did that happen just today?

Moe
Nope but you just heard about it today.

Joe
So does it count? As your daily play?

Moe
Under the circumstances it's ok by me.

Day 34: February 22

STANDING ROCK IS BURNING IN THE SNOW

Joseph
What are you doing?

Standing Rock Protester
I'm burning my teepee.

Joseph
'Cause the Army Corps is coming?

Standing Rock Protester
And we don't want them to touch anything that is sacred to us.

Joseph
But they're gonna make that pipeline.

Standing Rock Protester
Bury my heart at Standing Rock.

They continue to burn teepees.
The fire looks like a beacon.
Maybe it is.

Day 35: February 23

CAITLYN AND DONALD = ?

Caitlyn
Hi, I'm Caitlyn Jenner.

Joe
You mean Bruce Jenner?

Caitlyn
Now I identify as Caitlyn.

Joe
Ok.

Caitlyn
And I just want to say that I'm more than happy to explain transgender issues to the 45th because, as a wealthy white woman, who voted for him, I have a special perspective.

Joe
Ok.

Caitlyn
I'm also an actress, and would love to be in the play that's being written right now.

Joe
Ma'am you're deep up in it already.

Day 36: February 24

FROM RUSSIA WITH LOVE

Hank
The Russian flag is red, white and blue.

Joe
A lot of people don't know that.

Hank
So they passed out Russian flags with Trump's name on them.

Joe
Can you see it? Red, white and blue. /

Hank
/ With Trump in golden letters emblazoned on it. /

Joe
/ Distributed as flags to Trump supporters. /

Hank
/ And people walking around proudly waving them.

Joe
You're fucking kidding.

Hank
Nope.

Joe
And once again this isn't really a play.

Hank
We're shaking things up, Joe.

Joe
Oh.

Day 37: February 25

MUHAMMAD ALI, JR. GETS DETAINED AT THE FORT LAUDERDALE, FLORIDA, AIRPORT

TSA Person
Are you a Muslim?

Muhammad Ali, Jr.
It's illegal to ask that.

TSA Person
Ok. How about this one? Where did you get your name?

Muhammad Ali, Jr.
From my dad.

TSA Person
Why did he name you Muhammad Ali?

Muhammad Ali, Jr.
He named me after himself. I'm Muhammad Ali, Jr.

TSA Person
So your father is a Muslim.

Muhammad Ali, Jr.
Yes. Was.

TSA Person
What did he do for a living?

Muhammad Ali, Jr.
He was a fighter.

TSA Person
Aha! An enemy combatant!

Muhammad Ali, Jr.
No. A boxer.

TSA Person
He hit people.

Muhammad Ali, Jr.
He was Muhammad Ali, fool!

TSA Person
Step this way, come with me.

Muhammad Ali, Jr.
What for?

TSA Person
You're suspicious.

And in that moment:
The Amazing and Awesome Muhammad Ali rises from the grave
and treats us to one more knock-out punch,
but not to the lowly TSA agent.
Muhammad Ali, The Greatest,
punches The Man square in the face.
And The Greatest has just truly Made America Great Again.

Day 38: February 26

LA LA LA FANTASY

CNN
And the winner of the election is:

FOX
Hillary Clinton by 50 million votes. Oh shit lemme do that again.

CNN
And the winner of the presidential election is:

FOX
Donald Trump.

CNN
Not the popular vote.

FOX
But the electoral college.

CBS, NBC and ABC
Wait there's been a mistake: The true real winner is Hillary!

Hillary and the Whole Wide World
Yay!

Jack
Wake up.

Jill
I'm living the American Dream.

Jack
No, Trump really won! He's our new president.

Jill
But they mis-announced the winner of the Best Picture Oscar. It was really *Moonlight* but they said *La La Land.*

Jack
This ain't a movie, Jill.

Jill turns off the TV and the world goes dark.
Stay tuned.

Day 39: February 27

THE 45TH IS NOT RESPONSIBLE FOR THE SHOOTINGS IN KANSAS CITY

The 45th
People named Sean should be slapped.

FOX News
People named Sean should be slapped.

Angry Mobs
We are being told that people named Sean should be slapped.

The 45th
It'll make America slap again.

Joe from Kansas City walks up to Sean Spicer and slaps him.
Sean Spicer slaps Joe back. This goes on for a while.

May
This is an outrage! Someone needs to be locked up. Right?

Jane
Woah! Press Secretary Sean Spicer?

Sean Spicer
Yes?

Jane
Does your getting slapped have anything to do with what the president said?

Sean Spicer
Connecting my getting slapped to the words of the 45th President is just absurd.

Jack
You bet it's absurd.

Jill
Can I turn the television back on?

Day 40: February 28

BETSY DEVOS NEEDS TO BE TAKEN TO SCHOOL

Jack
She sent out a letter praising historic black colleges for being a great example of choice-educational opportunities.

Jill
'Cause she's completely clueless that they were founded because black people were *outlawed* from attending white schools!

Jack and Jill
Betsy DeVos. Somebody oughta take you to school!

George Washington
Has it come to this?

Abe Lincoln
'Fraid so, George, 'fraid so.

Day 41: March 1

EATING SHIT

Jack
Look, the media is eating shit.

Jill
Yeah, the 45th just gave his speech to Congress and they're eating it up.

Jack
Shit.

Jill
No shit.

Day 42: March 2

R-E-C-U-S-E

Cheerleaders
R-E-C-U-S-E! That's the word for Jeff to be!

Newsperson
Today, Attorney General Jeff Sessions recused himself from the Russia inquiries involving the Trump administration.

Translator
Translation: Our new Attorney General Jeff Sessions 1. Lied under oath saying he'd not had contact with the Russian Government last year and, in fact, he had contacted them *twice*, and 2. He's just admitted he cannot be impartial during the Russia inquiry.

Jack
Is he going down?

Jill
I'm taking a wait-and-see attitude.

Day 43: March 3

A MAN TAKING HIS KIDS TO SCHOOL IS ARRESTED BY ICE

Man
I'm just walking my kids to school.

ICE Agents
What are you doing?!

Man
Walking my kids to school.

Kids
This is our dad.
This is our school.
We are all walking there.

Boy Kid
I just farted.

ICE Agents
You're under arrest! Come with us!
You're an undocumented person!

They haul the Man away.
His Kids burst into tears.
This really happened today.
In America.

Day 44: March 4

BUGGY

The 45th
He's bugging me!
That's why there are all the leaks
All the freaks
All the sheiks
Taking leaks
With the geeks

He's tapping my phone
I don't wanna go home
My golden shower
I mean my golden home
Is bugging
Obama, why are you bugging me?

Jack
45th is bugging.

Jill
It's a very stressful job.

Day 45: March 5

IT'S THE BLACK GUY'S FAULT!

The 45th
The black guy is spying on me! He's tapping my phones, he's taking my shit, he's the cause of all my problems!

FBI Director
What black guy, Mr. 45th?

The 45th
The—Muslim black guy!

FBI Director
Be more specific.

The 45th
Obama, the 44th President.

FBI Director
You're going to have to publicly deny that, sir. You don't have any evidence.

The 45th
You were on my side before the election. When you—right before the election you said some shit about Hillary. That was for me, right?

FBI Director
No comment.

Day 46: March 6

STANDING GUARD

American Muslim
Hi there, my name is Ali. I'm an American Muslim. And also a war veteran. A marine. From Chicago.

American Jew
What are you doing here at the cemetery in broad daylight?

American Muslim
I'm standing guard. I've joined with a lot of other service people around the country to stand guard over Jewish houses of worship and other Jewish sacred places. To make sure that they are not vandalized.

American Jew
That's very—American of you.

American Muslim
That's very much—the idea.

Day 47: March 7

YOUR IPHONE INSTEAD OF YOUR HEALTH CARE

Jason Chaffetz (R-Utah)
I'm Jason Chaffetz (R-Utah). Poor people should quit buying iPhones then they could afford health care!

News Reporter
Did you really just say that?

Jason Chaffetz (R-Utah)
I really just said that. Want me to say it again?

News Reporter
Sure. For the record.

Jason Chaffetz (R-Utah)
I'm Jason Chaffetz (R-Utah) and folks could afford health care if they just quit buying iPhones.

Jack
Hello?!

Jill
It's a game of telephone. The words just sound stupider and make less sense every time you hear them.

Day 48: March 8

LADY LIBERTY'S LIGHTS WENT OUT

Children's Choir
Lady Liberty's lights went out
On the International Day without a Woman
On the day women
All around the world

Went on strike
Protesting
Widespread unfairness.

Lady Liberty's lights went out
Google it if you don't believe it
Dark she stood there
In the darkness
When she *used* to always
Light the way
And hold the light.

Lady Liberty's lights went out
The National Park Service, in charge of such things
They said it was a technical malfunction
Maybe, but hey
Lady Liberty is down with the struggle
True dat. Peace out.

Day 49: March 9

NOT MUCH

JD
I'm from the Justice Department.

Jack
Great! The 45th alleges that Obama wiretapped him.

JD
Yep.

Jill
So either it's true or the 45th has indicated that he's being investigated, that he's the subject of an investigation.

Jack
Is the 45th being investigated?

Sean Spicer
I'm Sean Spicer. And, nope, the 45th isn't being investigated.

Jill
Is the 45th being investigated?

JD
Uh—no comment.

Jill
No comment?!

Jack
Woah.

Sean Spicer
This isn't much of a play.

Jill
He isn't much of a president.

May
How dare you say that!!!

Day 50: March 10

SOS

Sean Spicer
This is Sean Spicer, the president's press secretary here again blah blah blah blah . . .

Jack
His lapel! Look!

Jill
He's wearing his lapel pin, the American flag—

Jack and Jill
Upside-down.

Jill
Wearing the flag upside-down is a sign of distress—SOS.

Jack
Think he needs help?

Jill
Maybe.

Sean Spicer
Woopsy!

He turns his lapel pin right side up.

Jill
He so needs help.

Day 51: March 11

AGAIN NO GAIN

Newscaster
After testifying about being detained at the airport under suspicion of having a suspicious name, when he flew home, Muhammad Ali's son was detained at the airport again.

Jack
He was detained again?!

Believer
Muhammad Ali, the famous boxer's son. Yeah. He's got a suspicious name.

Fever
Didn't you write this play already?

Jill
It happened again so we're writing it again.

Jack
Write on.

Day 52: March 12

U.S. ATTORNEY PREET BHARARA DIDN'T RESIGN

"Moments ago I was fired." —Preet Bharara.

Preet Bharara
Hey I'm U.S. Attorney Preet Bharara, Attorney General in the State of New York. The current administration wants to get rid of me. I'm standing up to him.

Jeff Sessions
Resign and go quietly.

Preet Bharara
I will not.

The 45th
You're fired!

U.S. Deputy Attorney General Sally Yates
Welcome to the club.

Day 53: March 13

MY 5-YEAR-OLD SON HAS A DREAM

Durham
Last night I was dreaming about Donald Trump.

Dad
Yeah?

Durham
And we all were in a play.

Mom
Really?

Durham
And, in the play, I didn't understand why he was president. So we all became Ninja Turtles and we went out for pizza.

Mom and Dad
Cool.

Day 54: March 14

PI IN THE FACE

Jack
Happy Pi Day.

Jill throws a pie in Jack's face.

Jill
Today was a snow day. Our kids stayed home from school and someone got their hands on the 45th's tax returns from 2005.

Jack
It's a snow job, People.

Jack and Jill
RESIST!

Day 55: March 15

NO WIRETAP, K?

FBI
There is no evidence of any wiretapping of Trump Tower by anyone.

Jack
Why's the Spokesperson got her head in the microwave?

Spokesperson
'Cause microwaves can be used as surveillance devices.

Jill
What makes the Spokesperson think that anybody wants to listen in to anything she's saying?

May
You all should be ashamed of yourselves! Bad mouthing them like that. You need to give them a chance!

Day 56: March 16

CLOWNS

Ronald McDonald
Hi, I'm Ronald McDonald and on Twitter today I tweeted: "President Trump you are actually a disgusting excuse of a president and we would love to have Barack Obama back. Also you have tiny hands."

Jack
They say it wasn't the real Ronald McDonald that tweeted that about the real Donald.

Jill
We got a real clown in the White House though. And that ain't no joke.

Ronald McDonald
True dat.

Day 57: March 17

I HAVE AN APPOINTMENT WITH THE PRESIDENT

Guy
Hey there I'm a guy who's just scaled the wall at the White House. I've got an appointment with the president.

Secret Service
We're Secret Service. We gotta apprehend you.

Jack
17 minutes pass while trained Secret Service try to catch the guy.

Jill
While we haven't yet seen photos of the guy, I'm guessing he was not a colored person, else they would've shot him. 'Cause if ever they could have cause to "Stand Your Ground," like, now's the time, right?

Jack
Meanwhile, in New York City, a Secret Service member's laptop is stolen.

Jill
Secret Service Shitstorm!

Day 58: March 18

SENDING LOVE TO CHUCK BERRY

Jill
Chuck Berry was the great soul-brother, the rock-and-roller, who wrote hits like "Roll Over Beethoven" and "Johnny B. Goode." He died today at 90 years old.

Jack
Google him. Just to see him strut with his guitar.

Jill
Also google Sister Rosetta Tharpe, who played in a similar style before Berry did. Both are awesome.

The 45th
I'm the 45th President and I'm lodging a complaint because this play doesn't have anything to do with me!!!

Jack and Jill
Exactly.

Day 59: March 19

3 SCARES? IN 8 DAYS?

Last night another person was taken into custody. For threatening the White House. It was the third threat in over a week.

Secret Service
At approximately 12:43 P.M. an individual jumped over the White House fence. Criminal charges are pending.

Jack
Is that the same guy who stole the laptop?

Jill
No, that was another incident.

Secret Service
If anyone has information on that laptop, give us a call.

Day 60: March 20

YES, THE 45TH IS BEING INVESTIGATED BY THE FBI

FBI Director
Hey there, I'm FBI Director James Comey.

Jack and Jill
We hate you.

FBI Director
How come, now?

Jack and Jill
'Cause you spread some shit about Hillary's emails a few days before the election and that didn't help things.

FBI Director
Yeah, my bad on that.

Jack and Jill
So we hate you.

FBI Director
Fair enough but I have some news that could maybe brighten up your day.

Jill
Go ahead. My day needs brightening.

FBI Director
It's the first day of spring!

Jack
Yeah, I really need the FBI to tell me that.

FBI Director
No, seriously, folks: The FBI is in fact investigating the 45th.

Jack and Jill
Seriously?

FBI Director
Seriously.

Jack and Jill
Should we wait to have a party?

FBI Director
That's up to you guys.

Jack and Jill
We trust you as far as we can throw you.

FBI Director
Which isn't far. I realize I have a credibility issue.

Jack and Jill
Life is short. Let's party.

They open paper sacks and take out paper hats, streamers, and noisemakers. It's a festive scene. After all it is the first day of spring and there are some things that even difficult times can't take away. Remember that.

Day 61: March 21

FOLLOW THE MONEY

Jack
The 45th owes over 300 Large to the Russian mob.

Jill
Preet Bharara was investigating this.

Jack
A Russian lawyer was scheduled to testify

Jill
But he fell off a building today.

The 45th
So?

Jack and Jill
We're following the money.

Day 62: March 22

CLINGS TO HIS ASSERTIONS LIKE A DRUNK TO HIS EMPTY GIN BOTTLE

The 45th
I'm the 45th President.

Jack
The *Wall Street Journal* says the 45th is his "own worst political enemy." That he's damaging his presidency with "his seemingly endless stream of exaggerations, evidence-free accusations, implausible denials and other falsehoods."

Jill
Ouch.

Jack
They go on, saying that he "clings to his assertions like a drunk to his empty gin bottle."

Jill
Ouch ouch.

The 45th
But, I don't even drink!

Jack
The *Wall Street Journal* goes on, saying, if he doesn't show more respect for the Truth, most Americans may conclude that he's a fake president.

The 45th
Ouch.

Jill
Ouch, Ouch. Ouch, Ouch.

Day 63: March 23

FORMER RUSSIAN MEMBER OF PARLIAMENT, DENIS VORONENKOV, WAS SHOT DEAD IN BROAD DAYLIGHT

Jack
Former Russian MP, Denis Voronenkov, an outspoken opponent of Vladimir Putin, was shot dead outside a hotel today. He had fled to Kiev in fear of his life and to help with inquiries into Russia's incursions into the Ukraine.

The 45th
I thought your plays were going to be about me? This doesn't have anything to do with me.

Jill
It will. Just wait.

Day 64: March 24

ART OF THE DEAL—NOT

Jack
Republicans admit defeat of their Trumpcare Health Bill.

Jill
How ya feeling?

Jack
Great.

Day 65: March 25

BECAUSE

Jack
But, Mr. President, your—Alternative Facts—

The 45th
"I must be doing a great job because—I'm the president and you're not."*

Jill
Did he really just say that?

Jack
Yup.

* He really said that.

Day 66: March 26

SHOW ME THE MONEY

The 45th
Here's a 374-billion-dollar invoice. I'm handing it to Germany, 'cause they owe us money for NATO.

Chancellor Angela Merkel
Er spinnt! Er weiss nicht wie NATO funktioniert.

Jill
(As translator) Ummmm. He doesn't know how NATO works.

Jack
45th, how about having a handshake with the German Chancellor?

The 45th
I won't shake her hand but I will hand her this invoice.

Chancellor Angela Merkel
Er ist Dick und Doof.

Jill
(As translator) He's like people on television.

Jack
Nuff said.

Day 67: March 27 (Play #1)

HE CALLS LOSSES WINS

Jack
Studies show that repeating a lie can make it seem more credible.

Jill
Lie
Tie
Tre
Tru.

Another play on the same day:

Day 67: March 27 (Play #2)

DICK CHENEY ON BOARD

Dick Cheney
Hi, I'm Dick Cheney. I'm the former VP. I have someone else's heart. Two things quickly:

1. No doubt Russia interfered with our election.
2. Russian interference is an act of war.

The 45th
So maybe we should go to war with Russia. What does FOX News say?

Jack
Help. Somebody help. Who will help us?

Day 68: March 28

COAL AND MY PERSONALS

Man
Hi, I'm a coal miner.

Woman
And I'm a coal miner's daughter.

Jack
They're celebrating 'cause the 45th just signed an executive order undoing policies to fight climate change.

Man
Not sure it'll help the coal industry.

Woman
But here's hoping.

Jill
Plus, didn't Congress overturn a rule requiring internet providers to ask permission before selling consumers' personal data?

Jack
Yep.

Jill
I feel sick.

Day 69: March 29

A PLAY FOR MICHAEL SHARP ON MY MOTHER'S 80TH BIRTHDAY

Michael Sharp
Happy Birthday, Mrs. Parks.

Mrs. Parks
Thank you, young man. Who are you?

Michael Sharp
I'm Michael Sharp. I used to work for the United Nations. Recently I was in the Congo. Talking with people who were at war. Encouraging them to build rapport with each other. Then they reported me missing. Then they found my remains in a shallow grave.

Mrs. Parks
You were investigating human rights abuses and you were killed.

Michael Sharp
Yes, ma'am. But, you know, I still believe that one can always listen. You can always listen to people who want a chance to talk about how they see the world.

The 45th
You should be writing plays about me.

Mrs. Parks
You should be ashamed of yourself, sir.

Day 70: March 30

MICHAEL FLYNN WANTS IMMUNITY

Jack
Michael Flynn wants immunity then he says he'll testify.

Jill
Where there is smoke there is fire.

Jack
I'll ask him outright. Michael Flynn, did you do wrong?

Michael Flynn
I'm not going to answer that unless you agree not to punish me if I did.

Jack
Senate Intelligence Committee says no way.

Jill
Is "Senate Intelligence" an oxymoron?

Jack
I hear you. And let's also remember that, in 2016, Flynn said that "people who've been granted immunity have probably committed a crime."

Day 71: March 31

THE ATTORNEY GENERAL IS WORRIED ABOUT WHITE VOTER INTIMIDATION

Jeff Sessions
I'm Jeff Sessions, the Attorney General. I'm making the intimidation of white voters my top concern, folks.

Jill
White voters are being intimidated?

Jeff Sessions
That's right and I'm going to make it my mission as Attorney General to find out why, and put an end to it. Any questions?

Jack
I want to rant and rave. Can I?

Jill
Let's.

They rant and rave.

Day 72: April 1

APRIL FOOL

The 45th
I'm here to sign 2 executive orders. They're very important. They're very very important. So let's sign them!

Jill
I'll provide the commentary, 'cause here's what happened next: The 45th steps away from the podium, smiles, and exits the room. His followers look on, totally dismayed

'cause he just left the room, forgetting to sign the executive orders which sit on his desk. Unsigned.

Jack
April Fools'? Nope. This really happened!*

* Yep. This really really happened.

Day 73: April 2

EPIC FAILURE

The 45th
The only thing that's happened is that I've signed executive orders.

Jack
That's a sign of a failed and stalled presidency.

The 45th
Shut up! That's an order!

Day 74: April 3

STUPID SUPREME

Sean Spicer
It's really sad that some senators are playing politics and not agreeing to vote on the confirmation of a Supreme Court nominee.

Jack
Isn't that exactly what the Republicans did last year?

Jill
Definitely pot calling the kettle black.

Sean Spicer
We might have to go nuclear.

Jack and Jill
Jeez.

Day 75: April 4

EVERYTHING AND NOTHING

Jill
Dr. Martin Luther King, Jr., was assassinated on this day, April 4th, 49 years ago.

Jack
Join hands, People. Join hands.

The 45th
I have tiny hands, so what does this have to do with me?

Jack
Everything.

Jill
And nothing.

Day 76: April 5

3 SURPRISES

Jack
Barry Manilow just came out as gay.

Jill
Duh.

(Rest)

Jill
GOPers wanna reform taxes but the 45th won't release his tax returns.

Jack
Jeez.

(Rest)

Jack
And the 45th regularly kisses his grown daughter on the lips.

Jill
Really?

May
Really? That can't be true. Really?

Jack
Which of these 3 surprises you most?

May
Can I answer that?

Jill
We're moving on, May.

Day 77: April 6

BLAME THE BLACK WOMAN

The 45th
Forget investigating my contacts to Russia, instead, investigate the fact that Susan Rice, former National Security Adviser, when she was National Security Adviser, was asking that folks, talking inappropriately to Russia, should be unmasked.

Jack
The job of National Security Adviser is to unmask people when they're behaving inappropriately.

The 45th
There's the smoking gun!

Jill
Yeah, 'cause her findings revealed that *you* were talking inappropriately to Russia.

Jack
He just implicated himself.

Jill
Yep.

Day 78: April 7

BOMBS AWAY

Jill
The U.S. just laid some air strikes on Syria.

Jack
Supposedly because Syria allegedly attacked its own civilians with nerve gas.

Jill
This Syria crisis is conveniently directing our attention away from creepy Supreme Court nominees, Attorney General rolling back police reforms, the gutting of the EPA and National Park Service, the list goes on and on.

Jack
Not much of a play.

Jill
Best she could do today, man.

Day 79: April 8

A SOLDIER WAS KILLED TODAY

Jack
A U.S. soldier was killed in action while conducting operations against ISIS in Afghanistan. The soldier was mortally wounded late Saturday.

Jill
We did not know you.
We will miss you.
We weave the strands of your life into our own.

Jack
They have yet to release the soldier's name.

Day 80: April 9

ONE MILLION DOLLARS PER MISSILE

CNN
The 45th bombed Syria! He just became president for real!

Jack and Jill
That is a pathetic stunt.

Jill
The 45th ordered 59 missiles dropped.

Jack
Do you know how much each missile costs?

Jill
1 million dollars per missile.

Jack and Jill
1 million dollars per missile.

Repeat that line forever or, you know, just long enough for it to really sink in.

Someone
Even if you're woke, wake up again, People!

Day 81: April 10

GUSH

News Anchors: Conservative and Progressive Alike
Gush gush gush gush gush gush gush gush gush gush gush gush gush gush gush.

Jack
What's the name of today's play?

Jill
Today's play is called *Gush*.

News Anchors
Gush gush gush gush gush gush gush gush gush gush.

Jack
What's the subject of the play?

Jill
How shit rises. How mediocre behavior and lame efforts are rewarded. How fairly intelligent folks gush over fair-to-midlin shit.

News Anchors
Gush gush gush gush gush.

Jack
The 45th bombed Syria.

Jill
And now everybody's gushing over him.

Jack
Got it.

News Anchors
Gush gush gush gush gush.

This action and these words will unfortunately
continue for a long time.
Yikes, but that's the way it is.

Day 82: April 11

HAPPY PASSOVER

Sean Spicer
Hey there, Sean Spicer here again. I'm the White House Press Secretary. Just wanna hip you guys to why we recently bombed Syria. 'Cause they're bad guys. Worse than Hitler. 'Cause, hey, even "Hitler didn't sink to the level of using chemical weapons on his people."

Jill
What?

Jack
What about the millions of Jews Hitler and his regime gassed?

Sean Spicer
He took them to "Holocaust Centers."

Jill
"Holocaust Centers"?

Sean Spicer
And Hitler, he didn't drop bombs on them, ok!

Jill
Is this how he celebrates Passover? By passing over?

Jack
He needs to resign. Now.

Day 83: April 12

JUDGE SHEILA ABDUS-SALAAM IS FOUND DEAD IN THE HUDSON RIVER

Jill
She was a black woman and a Muslim and a judge.

Jack
She was awesome, fair-minded, progressive.

Jill
She was found dead in the river.

The 45th
I'm starting to turn on Steve Bannon. Write a play about that.

Jill
Shut up. Rest in peace, Judge Sheila. You were a force for good.

Day 84: April 13

M.O.A.B.

The 45th
We dropped M.O.A.B., aka "The Mother of All Bombs" on ISIS today.

Jack
I thought Moab was a beautiful town in Utah. Blue skies, orange rocks. That natural rock arch.

The 45th
I promised to bomb the S-H-I-T out of ISIS. And I'm doing it. And—

Jill
And as long as we keep bombing things, people won't ask him about the racism, or the incompetence, or the ties with Russia.

Day 85: April 14, Good Friday

MISSED

Head of ISIS
That M.O.A.B.
It missed us.
So there.

Jack
Why are you wearing a ski mask?

Head of ISIS
Hiding my identity.

The 45th
We missed or we hit.
Either way, ISIS, you're helping me.

Head of ISIS
How so?

The 45th
My people. They hate you. I bomb you. They love me.

Jill
Who will help us?

Day 86: April 15

SHOW US THE MONEY

CNN
Hundreds of thousands around the country hit the streets in protest today demanding that the 45th President do as all other presidents have done and disclose his taxes.

The 45th
I don't want to. So there. 'Cause they will show—things I don't want you to see. But pretend that I just didn't say that, and you can't prove any of that, so there.

Hundreds of Thousands
Release your taxes!

The 45th
I'm going to bomb another country instead, ok? OK!

Day 87: April 16

ROLL AWAY THE STONE

The 45th
Happy Easter and welcome to the Easter egg hunt.

The Military Band plays the National Anthem.
The 45th just stands there smiling.

Wife of the 45th
Put your hand over your heart, dear, they're playing the National Anthem.

The 45th puts his hand over his heart.

The 45th
It's all in the details, isn't it?

Jack
Who will save us?

Jill
Don't hold your breath.

The 45th
Another lousy play.

Jack
Another lousy president.

Day 88: April 17

HATE LEADS TO DEPRESSION

Jack
I'm exhausted.

Jill
Me too.

Jack
At least we are in this together.

Jill
Are we?

Jack
Pretty much.

Jill
If the shit hits the fan will you split?

Jack
Probably.

Jill
I want to weep but I can't. I feel like I am saving my tears for something. I don't know what. The death of something closer to home, maybe. Some good news, news so good and touching that it will make me cry. Or I could cry now. Cry now and just get it over with. Or I could wait. I want to be able to fully cry when the really sad moment comes. And I don't know when that will be. Soon, I'll bet. And then all the tears, those of sadness and joy and anger will rush out of my body and flood the world, and they will say it was all because of climate change, or it wasn't.

Day 89: April 18

A SHOUT-OUT TO JON OSSOFF WHO ALMOST WON

Jack
Jon Ossoff almost won the congressional seat in Georgia.

Jon Ossoff
We didn't win but we beat the odds.

Jill
I feel a sense of despair.

Jon Ossoff
Feel it and then let it go. Despair is a wake-up call. We're working on this. You're not alone.

Day 90: April 19

WAITING FOR 4/20

Jill
I dunno. What's wrong with me?

Jack
What do you mean?

Jill
I've lost my joie de vivre.

Jack
Jill

Jack
Today is 4/19. 10 days to go with this project. 100 plays for the first hundred days.

Jill
Today's 4/19?

Jack
Yep.

Jill
Which means tomorrow's 4/20.

Jack
And we will get so baked.

The 45th
And will you be thinking of me?

Jill
Not. So not.

Day 91: April 20

NEW LOW

Jack and Jill smoke some weed from a lovely vape.

Jill
Over the past few years weed has been legalized in several states.

Jack
It's the least addictive substance

Jill
Less addictive than alcohol—and alcohol is legal.

Jack
The people in Washington are trying to make weed illegal again.

Jill
Happy 4/20! And welcome to an all new low.

Day 92: April 21

RIDICULOUS

The 45th
Before becoming president I promised to do a lot of really big things in my first 100 days in office. But now—I mean, what a ridiculous deadline, right?

Jill
4 out of 10 people say nothing he can or can't do will change their support of him.

Jack
Ridiculous.

Day 93: April 22

HAPPY EARTH DAY

Earth
Hi I'm the Earth. I don't look like how I'm usually represented. All those greens and blues and swirling clouds. This is me on the inside. And, on the inside, I'm actually kind of plain. I don't get out much. And, for all I give, I don't get much respect. Or love. Right now, People, I've got a message. /

The 45th
/ Hi I'm the president. I don't look how I'm usually represented. All that orange. I'm actually—

Jill and Jack
Shut up. It's Earth Day! Let's listen to the Earth.

Day 94: April 23

WHAT WILL YOU DO WHEN IT'S OVER?

Jack
What will you do when it's over?

Jill
Will you look back and think of all the things you could've fixed?

Jack
Or will you just
Keep on keeping on
With your eyes shut.

Jill
Are we making a song out of this?

Jack
Maybe.

Jill
The first 100 days will be over soon. What will you do?

Jack
Stop appearing in these plays for one.

Jill
What else? Will you go on a news-fast forever? That's what I'll do. I'll never watch the news again.

Jack
I'm praying that aliens come and abduct me.

Jill
Word.

Day 95: April 24

SEVEN PEOPLE PART-TIME

The 45th
How's that investigation going?

Jack
Which one?

The 45th
The one looking into my possible ties to Russia.

Jill
The investigation team, it's staffed with seven people and they're all part-time employees. Michael Flynn, Roger Stone, Carter Page, Paul Manafort or Jared Kushner—none of them have been interviewed yet.

Jack
How can you have a real investigation with only seven part-time staffers?

The 45th
So it's going great then, right? Great!

Day 96: April 25

FORGET THE WALL

The 45th
Ok, so I promised a wall but what I gotta have before my first 100 days is a win. And I'm going to win with the budget. Because if I don't, then I won't have a win and, also, no small point, the government will shut down. Which, I guess would be bad or it'll maybe make me look bad, and so forget the wall. For now. I'll get to it later. After I go golfing this weekend. And after I go to England. Where I want to get a ride in a golden coach.

Jill
Is this a play? Well, we have been played, that's for sure.

Day 97: April 26

IT'S ALMOST OVER

Jill
It's almost over.

Jack
Thank goodness.

Someone
What's almost over?

Jill
The first 100 days.

Someone
And then come the *second* 100 days.

Jack
Shit.

Jill
THIS IS BAD, PEOPLE! THIS IS REALLY BAD!

Day 98: April 27

THE NEW DOOMSDAY CLOCK

Jill
A recent poll shows that if the election were held again today, the 45th would win and by an even bigger margin.

Jack
In another study, academics tell us that America has only a year to reverse its course or succumb to fascism.

Jill
The new Doomsday Clock begins its countdown today.

Jack and Jill
TICK TICK TICK TOCK.

They repeat the last line for a whole year.
They RESIST as necessary.
Then they'll see what happens.
Fingers crossed. Here's hoping.

Day 99: April 28

MY PRESIDENT/NOT MY PRESIDENT

Jack
The 45th is the most unpopular president in American history.

Jill
We've endured weeks of cultural chaos and his policies are unpopular. And while most people disapprove of him, plenty say they'd still vote for him. What?

Jack
But, this just in: a poll by FOX News says only 36% of registered voters would vote for him again.

Jill
There was a storm last night. Rain, lightning and thunder. I sat up in bed and cried. People have fought and died to make this country live up to its ideals now it's going to shit.

Jack
We have been going to shit for a very long time.

Day 100: April 29

A HOUSE DIVIDED WILL NOT STAND

Gary
(White male, 64) 100 days isn't even important and besides I'd give him an A+.

David
(White male, 79) Korea is going nuclear. We've gotta deal with that.

Jack
What about health care, women's rights, deporting good people, Muslim bans, civil rights, Russian treason, public schools?

Gary
The media hates him and the protestors against him, they are paid to protest.

Jill
Resist.

Day 101: April 30

NOW WHAT?

The action of this play is everything that happens from here through eternity.

Day 102: May 1

MAYDAY

The stage is dark, then a bit of light.

Jack
It's day 102. And what should we do?

Jill
We should do our bit. 'Cause doing our bit makes a spark of light.

Jack
And *that's* what is remembered. *That's* what people see in dark times when they look back. They see sparks of light that help them continue.

Jill
Sparks of light can give folks an example of righteous behavior.

Jack
Bravery in times of despair.

Jill
Justice in times of injustice.

Jack
Kindness in a time of cruelty.

Jill
Little sparks of light. That's what stars are.

Jack
That's what you make when you do your bit. You make a little spark of light.

Jill
And the star you make, it'll guide future travelers. So, hey, shine on.

End of Plays

❤❤❤

Epilogue: February 8, 2018

AMERICAN

This morning I'm waiting to get on my plane, a flight on American (Airlines). I'm going to Roanoke, Virginia, so that I can speak with some students and faculty and staff at Washington and Lee University (or "W&L" as their university is lovingly called).

1. The flight is delayed.
2. Over the airport intercom blasts an impossible-to-understand set of instructions telling us, the folks heading to Roanoke, which new gate to go to.
3. Oswaldo, who will be our flight attendant, comes to help. With his delicious accent, he tells us to head down a corridor.
4. We do as we're told.

We are about ten folks: a tall gorgeous white lady lawyer; three co-workers traveling together: a black dude with some very happening style, a bespectacled and gregarious white woman, who is apparently a huge LeBron James fan, like she knows his birthday and all his stats; and a genial man of Pakistani descent who is talking with his co-workers about his parents. These three co-workers live in Lynchburg, which they say is beautiful. They all work in the life insurance business. Other passengers include: a red-haired lady doctor and her elderly but spry mother; there's a stylish Asian college student who snaps selfies for her sorority sisters; and there are two white guys: our pilot and co-pilot. If this were a film there would be a righteous Facebook post about why the white guys always get cast as the pilots. But this is not a movie. This is a play in the sense that all the world is a stage, this is something real that's happening, just this morning specifically in the airport and on the tarmac of LaGuardia Airport, New York City. Oh yeah, there's another character in this: there's me, the black woman writer who has been asked to speak to the students of W&L about *Diversity*.

We walk down long cold corridors, and then down a very steep set of cement steps. We stand outside. We are boarded onto a little bus. It seems to take us in a neat circle and drop us off where we started, but the yellow-vested gate attendant assures us that we're exactly where we're supposed to be. We get off that bus and are herded onto another. Dragging our baggage behind us. We talk and joke. We make conversation. We all look so different, but we are all American, all American on American, and all heading to the same place.

I tell the lawyer lady that I've been asked to speak about *Diversity*. "Yes W&L needs that conversation," she says. She's an alum and on the board of trustees. "Folks at W&L and all over the world need to listen to each other. To know that giving a chance to someone else does *not* deprive you of your chance. That's just an illusion. I'm thinking that we all need to spend some time walking around in someone else's shoes. Maybe for a whole day that's what we could do."

We finally reach our new gate. And we are lined up to board the plane. It's been like two hours, and three busses, and three different lines, and carrying our baggage up steep flights of stairs in four different terminals. I'm exaggerating but it has been a kind of a pain in the butt. And the TSA person wants my boarding pass. And I cannot find it. I get frantic. I panic. I put my folder down on the boarding pass electronic checker so that I can frantically search my pockets. I've been holding my folder all this time because in it is the speech that I will give to the students and faculty and staff of W&L. I had originally planned a speech about the creative process. Then they asked me to add something about *Diversity*. I don't know what I'll say about *Diversity*, but I'm hoping something will come to me. But the bulk of the speech is good. And I'm holding it in my folder so as not to lose it and I've lost my boarding pass instead. The three TSA people are glowering at me because my folder is covering up the electronic boarding pass security checker-thing. And I panic some more. And then I see that they're smiling. Because my folder has a picture of Ganesh on it. Ganesh the Hindu deity with the head of an elephant and the body of a human. Ganesh, the remover of obstacles. And the three TSA folks, two white guys and a black woman, are all Ganesh fans.

I find my boarding pass. It's right in my hand. We all board. All ten of us passengers. The plane taxis and then takes off, rising above the clouds to where the sun is always shining. And I have one of those awakenings, on my way to W&L to talk to folks about *Diversity*. I know that underneath all of the anger and fear, I know that we were all born to find a way to come together. Our great mission in life is to find a way to overcome our apparent differences and to come together, to find our way back to the Union.

Named among *TIME* magazine's "100 Innovators for the Next Wave," Suzan-Lori Parks is one of the most acclaimed playwrights in American drama today. She is the first African-American woman to receive the Pulitzer Prize in Drama. She is a MacArthur "Genius" Award recipient, and in 2015 she was awarded the prestigious Gish Prize for Excellence in the Arts. She has received grants and awards from the National Endowment for the Arts, the Rockefeller Foundation, the Ford Foundation, the New York State Council on the Arts and the New York Foundation for the Arts. She is also a recipient of a Lila-Wallace—Reader's Digest Award, a CalArts/Herb Alpert Award in the Arts, the Windham-Campbell Prize for Drama, and a Guggenheim Foundation Fellowship. She is an alumna of New Dramatists and of Mount Holyoke College.

Parks's project *365 Days/365 Plays* (when she wrote a play a day for an entire year) was produced at more than seven hundred theaters worldwide, creating one of the largest grassroots collaborations in theater history. Her other plays include *Topdog/Underdog* (2002 Pulitzer Prize winner), *The Book of Grace*, *Unchain My Heart: The Ray Charles Musical*, *In the Blood* (2000 Pulitzer Prize finalist), *Venus* (1996 OBIE Award), *The Death of the Last Black Man in the Whole Entire World*,

PHOTO BY TAMMY SHELL

Imperceptible Mutabilities in the Third Kingdom (1990 OBIE Award, Best New American Play), *The America Play* and *Fucking A*. Her adaptation of *The Gershwins' Porgy and Bess* won the 2012 Tony Award for Best Revival of a Musical. Her latest play, *Father Comes Home from the Wars (Parts 1, 2 & 3)*—set during the Civil War—was awarded the 2014 Horton Foote Prize, the 2015 Edward M. Kennedy Prize for Drama Inspired by American History, and was a 2015 Pulitzer Prize Finalist.

Parks has written numerous screenplays, including *Girl 6* for Spike Lee, and she adapted Zora Neale Hurston's *Their Eyes Were Watching God* for ABC Television's Oprah Winfrey Presents. Other film work includes *Anemone Me* (produced by Christine Vachon and Todd Haynes). She has recently completed a film adaptation of Richard Wright's *Native Son*, directed by Rashid Johnson, and a film about Billie Holiday, slated to be directed by Lee Daniels.

Parks's first novel, *Getting Mother's Body* (Random House, 2003), is a novel with songs and is set in the West Texas of her youth.

Parks is currently performing Watch Me Work, a free, weekly, live-streamed writing workshop, open to artists of all disciplines. Her plays are published by Theatre Communications Group (TCG), Samuel French and Dramatists Play Service. She is also at work on a stage musical adaptation of the film *The Harder They Come*. Parks was the Residency One playwright at Signature Theatre for their 2016–2017 season, and her band was also in residence.

Parks teaches at New York University, and serves at The Public Theater as its Master Writer Chair. She credits her mentor James Baldwin for starting her on the path of playwriting. One of the first to recognize Parks's writing skills, Mr. Baldwin declared Parks "an astonishing and beautiful creature who may become one of the most valuable artists of our time."

Please visit suzanloriparks.com